SIR JOHN SOANE'S MUSEUM

DIVSARFVNSVS

# THE NORTH ITALIAN ALBUM
# DESIGNS BY A RENAISSANCE ARTISAN

Lynda Fairbairn

æ

SJSM

Published in the United Kingdom
by Azimuth Editions

Azimuth Editions
33 Ladbroke Grove, London W11 3AY, England
Design by Anikst Associates



British Library Cataloguing in Publication Data
(data applied for)
ISBN 1-898592-18-7

Typeset by Anikst Associates and Azimuth Editions
Printed by PJ Reproductions, London

COVER. North Italian Album, p.14. Cityscape.
FRONTISPIECE. North Italian Album, p.32. A repertory page with designs for vases.

## *The North Italian Album*

On the 14th of February 1891, Baron Henry von Geymüller wrote a letter to the President of the Royal Institute of British Architects for publication in the Journal of the Institute on 19th February asking to add to an earlier paper he had written on Bramante. He related how recently 'Mr J.W. Wild, the Curator of Sir John Soane's Museum, drew my attention to a volume of sixty eight drawings on vellum in the Museum which he thought to be interesting; and in fact this they are in a very high degree, for after close examination I have been able to recognise them with entire certainty as authentic sketches of Bramante. But at the same time I felt much perplexity as to their significance, and sure that this affirmation would be met, at first at least, by an incredulity easily understood'.[1] Geymüller had in fact been examining a volume which has come to be called the North Italian Album, and he explained his perplexity about the drawings, which betray in turn naivety and sophistication, by suggesting that they are a kind of architectural 'joke, like a hieroglyphic riddle', intended as a gift from Bramante to an *intarsiatore* (FIG.1).[2]

Art historians were not drawn to the Album by the Baron's comments until 1957 when Marcel Rothlisberger, following Geymüller, characterised the Album as 'patterns for intarsia craftsmen'.[3] He identified some of the buildings represented in the volume: the Colosseum, the Arch of Constantine, the Florentine baptistery, the *Tempio Malatestiano* in Rimini, the *Porta Palatina* in Turin and the *Torre della Milizia* in Rome. He recognised the baluster-spoke wheel on p.51 (FIG.8) as a quotation from Bernardo Prevedari's engraving of Bramante's design for *The ruined temple,* and he attributed the Album to the Lombard–Veneto circle of *circa* 1500. Although there have been numerous attributions and datings since then, the Album has never been systematically catalogued and studied. What follows is the author's attempt to unravel the hands and the sources in this complex group of drawings.

Meg Licht in 1970 attributed the Album to Nicoletto da Modena, whose supposed signature, *Nicholeto da Modena Ferrara*, on a vault in the Domus Aurea in Rome, located his activity in Modena and Ferrara.[4] She made the comparison between the putto caryatids on the throne on a *graffito* insignia with an enthroned Madonna and child signed NICHOLET in the Museo Civico in Padua and similar putti on fols 24–25 of the Album, and noted the use of *repoussoir* architectural elements in Nicoletto's work, which are also frequently found in the Album.

The attribution to Nicoletto and the function of the drawings was not challenged until Graziano Manni, also convinced of its Ferrarese origins, attributed the Album to Gherardo Costa, and dated it *circa* 1470–80.[5] This attribution is difficult to sustain, because although documents record him as active as a decorator in Ferrara between 1454–80, no graphic work by him has survived.

FIG.1 North Italian Album, pp.8–9. *Architectural compositions*. The design on p.8 is loosely based on Castello Sforzesco in Milan. The domes on the corner towers recall Leonardo's unexecuted project for the castle. The composition on p.9 has a tower, a vase for a *sgraffito* decoration on a façade, and a goldfinch (?) painted by the hand of a miniaturist.

2

3

### *The Rothschild Album*

In 1973, Licht attributed some of the drawings in a dismembered album in the Rothschild Collection in the Louvre to the same hand as the Master of the North Italian Album.[6] She characterised them as drawings for festivities or stage sets influenced by Filarete's architectural treatises. Examination of the drawings confirms Licht's suggestion that the North Italian Album and some of the drawings on vellum in the Rothschild album are certainly by the same hand.[7] The quality of the drawing varies considerably but the style within each type of subject is unified and the consistency of the contents argues for a single hand.

The Rothschild album contains drawings by several hands which can be assigned to three groups. The first can be dated to the first half of the 15th century, one of the drawings being attributed to a North Italian draughtsman of the early 15th century after Altichiero.[8] Another is close to a drawing of knights in the Lugt Collection,[9] which probably derives from a drawing for one of Pisanello's historical fresco cycles, like the tournament fresco in the Ducal palace in Mantua (FIG.2).[10] A second group is by an artist identified by Marzia Faietti as the Master of the Flagellation, whose figures and landscapes are associated with North Italian painting at the end of the 15th century.[11] The drawing of the *Flagellation* demonstrates that he studied Pollaiuolo's work (FIG.3). The third is the group of architectural drawings by the same hand as the Master of the North Italian Album including a tower and a frieze drawn by him on folios with drawings by the early 15th century hand.[12]

A fourth artist, possibly a miniaturist, added the animals, birds and fruit to many of the folios, described above, in the Rothschild album. The same hand added drawings of animals, birds and sculpture to some of the folios in the North Italian Album (FIG.15). He used the same materials, pigments and mediums as the North Italian master, a fact which suggests that they were contemporaries who worked together in a workshop.[13]

It seems that the corpus of material, divided at an unknown date between the Rothschild album in the Louvre and the North Italian Album at the Soane, originally contained a stock of both figurative and architectural images, collected in the workshop for use as models to stimulate ideas for designs or to show to patrons. The painterly hands of the first half of the fifteenth century in the first group record motifs from North Italian painting, especially the Lombard and Paduan works of Altichiero and Pisanello, while the drawings from the second half of the 15th century in the third group are predominantly architectural, possibly reflecting a tendency which grew in the 1470s when architectural settings often overshadowed narratives and became the main subject of paintings. When the material was separated, the figurative material and eight sheets with the more refined architectural drawings were collated as the Rothschild album in the Louvre and the remaining architectural and ornamental designs as the North Italian Album in the Soane.

FIG.2 Anonymous Italian, first half of the 15th century, after Pisanello, *Knights in combat*, Louvre, Rothschild Collection, inv.no.843DRV.

FIG.3 Master of the Flagellation, after Antonio Pollaiuolo, *The Flagellation of Christ*, Louvre, Rothschild Collection, inv.no.859DRV.

FIG.4 (opposite page) Master of the North Italian Album, p.56. *View of a bridge based on Ponte Sant'Angelo* in Rome. The putto on the right is derived from Donatello's *Atys*, while the little figure on the left is based on Riccio's *Tobias*.

FIG.5 Giovanni Marcanova, *Quaedam Antiquitatum Fragmenta*. A reconstructed view of the Mausoleum of Hadrian and Ponte Sant'Angelo in Rome. Modena, Biblioteca Estense, MS.lat.992, fol.39r.

### *Pattern books*

In general, several different types of artists' repertories or pattern-books survive, one of the finest being the erudite and beautiful *Codex Escurialensis* in the Escorial in Madrid, which shows views of Roman buildings as well as details of ornament which could be used by artists as exemplary models. It formed part of the material assembled by Philip II of Spain, when he was planning to build the Escorial, and was used to supply the example of Antiquity as an inspiration to architects and artisans who had not been to Rome. Others were like the refined sketchbook in the *Kunstbibliothek* in Berlin, by the Master of the Mantegna sketchbook of the 1460s and 70s, which was probably circulated between the artists and the artisans who served almost exclusively the Gonzaga Court at Mantua.[14] It contains variations on classical details, bases, capitals and entablatures, candelabra and vases arranged repetitively, which could be used as an authority for the design of classicizing details. It was made from drawings from Mantegna's studio,[15] which Leoncini suggested could have been made from original drawings of the 1450s by Filarete. Then there were the engravings, available for sale to artisans, like the single designs for pilasters by Zoan Andrea, who was trained in Mantegna's circle.

In the early drawings in the Rothschild album the masters selected a stock of images from other artists' designs for use in their own work, while the Master of the North Italian Album made repertory pages of single objects like vases (FRONTISPIECE), but more frequently he re-elaborated and interpreted contemporary architectural ideas and imaginatively turned them into compositions, which could be used whole or quoted as details. The designs are available for interpretation in many ways so that they can supply ideas to artisans in different trades for a variety of objects. For this reason the final destination of a design is not always readily definable; the design for the tabernacle (FIG.23) was used as the architectural setting in which the attic is opened as a balcony for the figures for the narrative in an engraving of *The Descent of the Spirit*,[16] or it was used for the brass case of an astrolabic clock (FIG.24).[17]

The identification of many of the subjects in both albums suggest that the drawings originated in Northern Italy, most probably in Milan, which was an international

6

FIG.6 Sperandio of Mantua. *Medal of Francesco Sforza*, d.1466. The building on the reverse is probably Filarete's unrealised project for Francesco Sforza's mausoleum. London, Victoria and Albert Museum, Department of Sculpture, A.201–1910.

FIG.7 Master of the North Italian Album, elevation of a centralized five-dome building based on Sperandio's medal. Louvre, Rothschild Collection, inv.no.858DR bisv.

city where the industrial arts were particularly well developed for the production of luxury goods. Artisans competed in Milan on the international market which served the Court of the Sforza, Dukes of Lombardy, Lombard nobility, foreign bankers and the municipality. They fulfilled the demands of a large aristocratic class, who bought from the stock in their shops in the city, as well as the needs of the Sforzas who were also frequently satisfied by shopping trips.[18] The Venetian ambassador's description of Milan in 1520 gives an outline of the situation:

'The city of Milan is large and has the highest population in all of Italy. There are many poor and they eat cornmeal. There is also a great quantity of gentlemen who

have incomes from eight to 10,000 ducats. They spend greatly on their households ... There is a great number of artisans, more than any other Christian city, who make every type of work and goods, which are exported throughout the world ... '[19]

The Milanese enjoyed furnishings and architectural ornament which were richly decorated with mouldings and with classical motifs. The portals of the city's palaces were framed in terracotta relief tiles with classicizing ornament derived from the classical repertory developed in Padua in the 1440s to 1460s during Donatello's residence in the city. Several images in the North Italian Album can be traced to Paduan sources.

FIG.8 North Italian Album p.51. *Cityscape.* A variant on the design on FIG.9, with the façade opened as a loggia.

FIG.9 (above, left) Master of the North Italian Album. *Cityscape.* A five-dome plan is inserted behind the façade of the church on the piazza shown on FIG.10. Louvre, Rothschild Collection, inv.no.858DRr.

FIG.10 (above, right) Attributed to Antonio Averlino, called Filarete, *Christ healing the possessed man.* Silver plaquette. Louvre, Département des Objets D'Art.

### *Paduan sources*

An important Paduan source, for example, was a manuscript in Modena entitled *Quaedam Antiquitatum fragmenta*, an illustrated corpus of classical inscriptions made between 1457 and 1460, which was collected by Giovanni Marcanova, 1410/18–1467,[20] a learned epigrapher and Doctor of Medicine who taught at Padua and who composed the inscription for Donatello's equestrian statue, *Gattamelata*, in Padua. It shows ancient Rome whimsically reconstructed, with complete buildings, obelisks and columns like large scale pieces of jewellery, as the romantic settings for the epigraphy. Dedicated in 1465 to Malatesta Novello,[21] the Lord of Cesena, it was transcribed and illustrated by the epigrapher and eccentric Felice Feliciano who worked for him as a scribe, and who made a copy of it for his friend Andrea Mantegna. In the view of the Mausoleum of Hadrian and Ponte Sant'Angelo (FIG.5) the tomb is shown with a drafted-masonry cubical basement and cylindrical upper storey like the building in FIG.18. The view down on to the bridge with two towers at either end of the bridge is close to FIG.4. The ornament with crenellations above machicolations, and the deeply carved classical dentils, and egg and dart mouldings in Marcanova's illustrations are also typical of the North Italian Album.[22]

The Master of the North Italian Album quoted from Mantegna's Paduan work very specifically in the drawing of a triumphal arch (FIG.12), which is taken from his fresco *Saint James led to Execution* in the funeral chapel of Antonio degli Ovetari in the church of the Eremitani in Padua.[23] The Master of the North Italian Album copied only a fragment from the fresco, the pier of a Roman arch with three reliefs of a ewer and rudder below a roundel suspended from a palm tree, a relief of a trophy and a charioteer relief in the cornice on the right, but the position of the relief of the palm tree and trophy are reversed,[24] and the roundel contains a Roman inscription in Mantegna's fresco. The relief in the drawing in the frieze above the pier on the left of the design shows a scene of sacrifice not shown in Mantegna's fresco. Two reliefs, however, in the attic of Nero's Palace in Filarete's *Martyrdom of St Peter* on the bronze doors of St Peter's show a sacrificial scene on the left and a figure in a chariot pulled by satyrs on the right,[25] like those in the drawing.

FIG.11 Andrea Mantegna, *St James led to Execution*. Padua, Chiesa degli Eremitani, Ovetari Chapel.

FIG.12 (opposite page) North Italian Album, p.15. *Triumphal arch*.

### *The influence of Filarete's Milanese architecture*

Several of the images in the Album relate to the work of architects working in Milan in the 1450s and 1460s. When Francesco Sforza became 2nd Duke of Lombardy in 1450, he established cultural and financial links with Florence and Piero de'Medici recommended Antonio Averlino, il Filarete, the Florentine architect and sculptor, who had worked in Rome and who came to Milan in the 1450s and was resident there from 1461 until 1469, as chief architect of the Cathedral, of the tower of Castello Sforzesco and of the Hospital. Michelozzo was also in Milan between 1462 and 1468 to build the Medici Bank and the chapel for Pigello Portinari in S.Eustorgio which were both modified by the local taste of the builders.

FIG.13 North Italian Album, pp.42–43. *Architectural compositions with a castle gate and the Colosseum set in a landscape.* The castle is loosely based on Castello Sforzesco in Vigevano. The entablature of the Colosseum rises in the centre in opposition to the laws of pespective; it probably derives from Francesco di Giorgio's illustration in his treatise. The colouring of the sky fading to yellow and pink and the rocky mountain recall Bramantino's paintings.

Filarete's architecture, especially the building on the reverse of Sperandio's medal of Francesco Sforza, which has been interpreted as Filarete's unrealized project for the centrally planned mausoleum that Francesco Sforza wanted to build, was also an important source for the draughtsman of the Album.[26] Typologically the building shown on the medal conforms with Filarete's five-domed schemes in his manuscript treatise.[27] One of the drawings by the Master of the North Italian Album, now in the Rothschild album in the Louvre, shows the building as it appears on the medal (FIG.7).

A related building is shown on another drawing by the Master of the North Italian Album, in the Rothschild album, in which a five-domed building is represented as a cross inscribed in a square behind a flat closed façade (FIG.9). This drawing is based on the beautiful silver plaquette in the Louvre of *Christ healing a possessed man* traditionally attributed to Brunelleschi (FIG.10).[28] In the relief the miracle takes place on a city square in front of a building with fluted pilasters supporting a deep entablature with a frieze of fat-cheeked putti and garlands,[29] aedicular portals below two domes with scallop-tiled roofs, crowned by lanterns. Isabelle Hyman, who noted the deliberate references in the relief to contemporary Florentine painting and sculpture in the narrative of the miracle, interpreted the architecture, like the figures, as deferential references to contemporary Florentine architecture of 1420–60, and to Florentine historical architecture. The marble revetment of the façade in the plaquette she relates to the Florentine baptistery or San Miniato al Monte.[30] The setting for the miracle is Piazza San Lorenzo in Florence; the plaquette shows the façade of the church, completed following a mid-15th century project, probably Michelozzo's, but the cruciform plan behind the façade, with the domed chapels in the crossing, which is typical of plans in Filarete's treatise,[31] does not correspond with the project for a Latin cross church. She suggested that the other buildings on the left were derived from Filarete's imperfect recollection of Alberti's Holy Sepulchre in the Rucellai chapel in San Pancrazio, the crenellated wall on the right as the garden wall of Palazzo Medici and the building on the left as Palazzo Medici, which was unfinished when Filarete left Florence. The way that it rises above the frame and the holes for scaffolding poles gives the building the air of Lombard brick towers. The arched lancets resting on the cornice of a tall basement she attributed to an imperfect memory of Brunelleschi's Palazzo di Parte Guelfa, which has oculi above the lancets.[32]

Hyman attributed the plaquette to Filarete, who trained as a goldsmith in Florence, and suggested that he made it as gift for the Medici after he left Florence. The choice of silver, a precious metal, for the Louvre plaquette, which bears traces of polychrome enamel, and the intricately wrought arabesque frame as well as the multiple undisguised references to Florentine art underpin its function as a tribute. The cityscape in the North Italian Album (FIG.8)is a variant of the composition showing the building with an open loggia, three bays wide and deep with five domes,

FIG.14 Circle of Michelozzo di Bartolomeo, 1396–1472. *A putto standing on a tortoise.* Abbott Guggenheim Collection, New York State.

FIG.15 (opposite page) North Italian Album p.55.

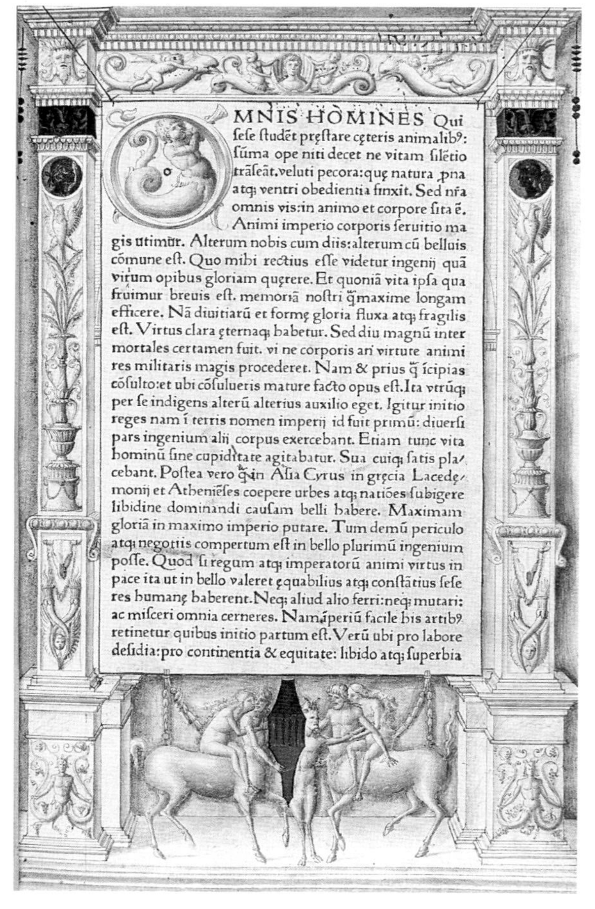

OMNIS HOMINES Qui
sese studēt prestare ceteris animalib9:
sūma ope niti decet ne vitam silētio
trāseāt. veluti pecora: que natura pna
atq; ventri obedientia finxit. Sed nr̄a
omnis vis: in animo et corpore sita ē.
Animi imperio corporis seruitio ma
gis utimūr. Alterum nobis cum diis: alterum cū belluis
cōmune est. Quo mihi rectius esse videtur ingenij quā
virum opibus gloriam querere. Et quoniā vita ipsa qua
fruimur breuis est. memoriā nostri q̄ maxime longam
efficere. Nā diuitiarū et forme gloria fluxa atq; fragilis
est. Virtus clara eternaq; habetur. Sed diu magnū inter
mortales certamen fuit. vi ne corporis ari virtute animi
res militaris magis procederet. Nam & prius q̄ ícipias
cōsulto: et ubi cōsulueris mature facto opus est. Ita vtrūq;
per se indigens alterū alterius auxilio eget. Igitur initio
reges nam í terris nomen imperij id fuit primū: diuersi
pars ingenium alij corpus exercebant. Etiam tunc vita
hominū sine cupiditate agitabatur. Sua cuiq; satis pla/
cebant. Postea vero q̄ in Asia Cyrus in grecia Lacede/
monij et Atheniēses coepere urbes atq; natiōes subigere
libidine dominandi causam belli habere. Maximam
gloriā in maximo imperio putare. Tum demū periculo
atq; negotiis compertum est in bello plurimū ingenium
posse. Quod si regum atq; imperatorū animi virtus in
pace ita ut in bello valeret equabilius atq; constātius sese
res humane haberent. Neq; aliud alio ferri: neq; mutari:
ac misceri omnia cerneres. Nam iperiū facile his artib9
retinetur quibus initio partum est. Verū ubi pro labore
desidia: pro continentia & equitate: libido atq; superbia

17a

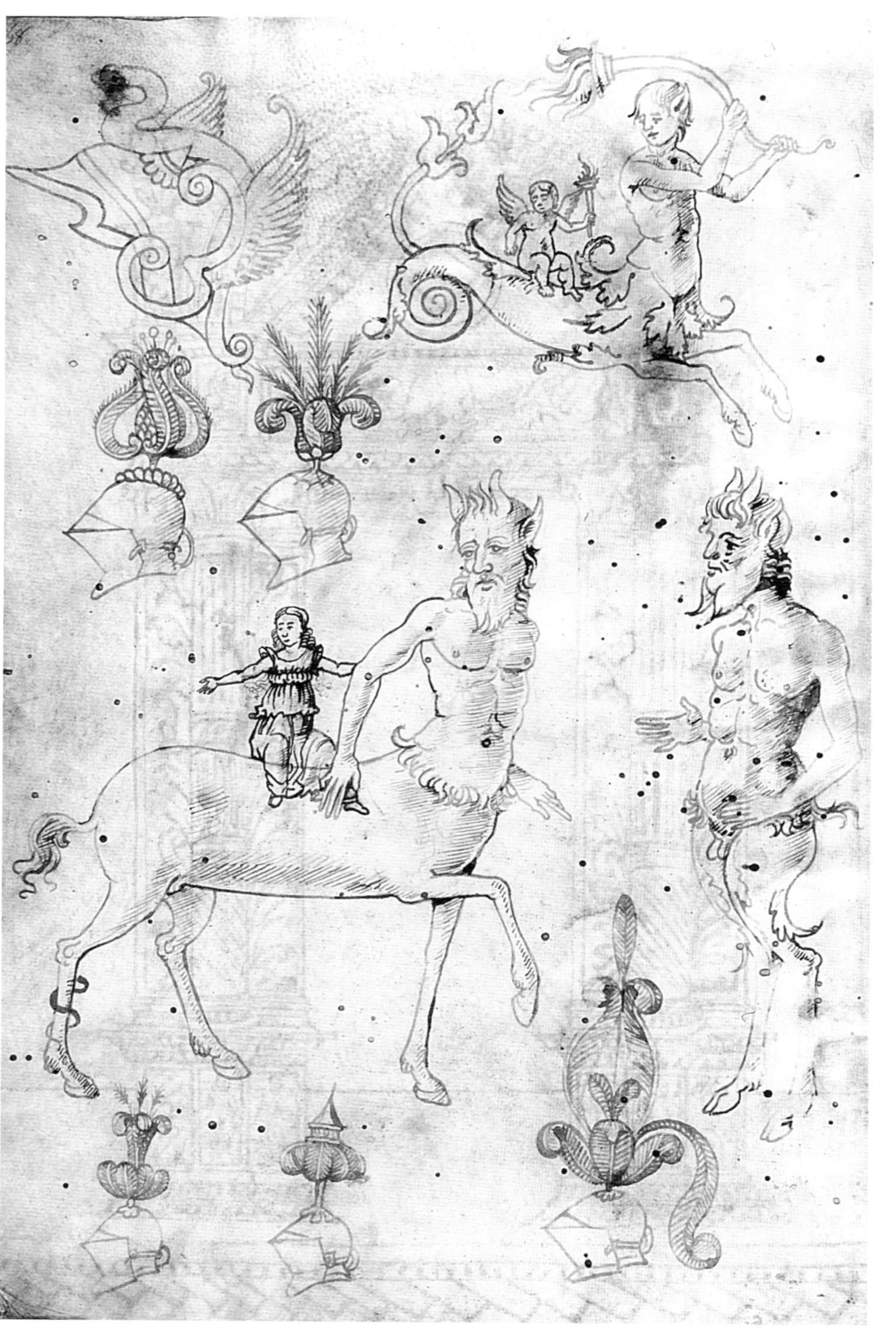

16

FIG.16 North Italian Album, p.68. *Nessus and Deianeira*. The centaur who abducted Deianeira from Hercules is shown as a thin elderly figure, like those by the London Pliny Master, with a satyr who has no role in the story.

FIG. 17a London Pliny Master. Sallust, *Opera*, Venice, J. De Colonia and J. Manthen, 1474, f.1. The John Rylands University Library, University of Manchester, inc.no.10547.

FIG. 17b (right) Detail of FIG. 17a

on a podium of steps in a piazza lined with noble palaces.[33] The image circulated widely in Lombardy, a cheaper version of the plaquette being cast in bronze; the many references to it in Milanese artefacts confirm her suggestion.

### *Small bronzes and manuscripts*

The birds, fruit and animals in the North Italian Album and on some of the pages of the Rothschild album, were possibly copied from a book of models; they could have been used to decorate manuscripts or Ducal diplomas. They are by our fourth artist, whose mastery over mixing and applying colour, which is superior to the architectural hand, suggests that he could be a miniaturist, who makes several explicit references to specific works of art. The standing putto holding an orb (FIG.15) derives from a bronze statuette of a *Putto standing on a tortoise* in the Abbott Guggenheim Collection in New York which Laura Cammins has convincingly dated *circa* 1440, and attributed to the circle of Michelozzo (FIG.14).[34] The putto in

the Album is not standing on a tortoise but he has the same braided hairstyle and sandals as Michelozzo's little bronze statuette, and he carries an orb or ball in his left hand which has probably been lost in Michelozzo's original.[35] The seated, winged putto on the right of the sheet is derived from the child in an oval marble relief attributed by Charles Avery to Donatello of the *Madonna and child* in the Victoria and Albert Museum.[36] The putto on the parapet in Schiavone's *Virgin and child* in the Galleria Sabauda in Turin is probably a winged relative of the same baby. This putto holds a book, a rare subject, although there are several examples in Paduan art: a putto by Bartolomeo Bellano, d.1497, sits holding a book on the architrave of the Sacristy at the *Santo* in Padua and three of the reliefs on the tomb of Girolamo and Marc'Antonio Dalla Torre by Riccio, formerly in San Fermo in Verona and now in the Louvre, dated between 1506–11, show standing winged putti with books.[37]

The mask on the pediment in the same sheet which is drawn by the Master of the North Italian Album, also seems to be a direct quotation from the mask of the

FIG.18 North Italian Album, pp.12–13. *Façade and a cityscape*. The overall scheme of the façade with a tall, crested basement, corner pilasters with the domed superstructure between corner pavilions on trabeated columns is derived from the Colleoni chapel (FIG.19). See *also* FIG.29.

FIG.19 BERGAMO, Colleoni chapel, the first Renaissance, free-standing, central-plan mausoleum of the 1470s, by Giovanni Antonio Amadeo.

FIG.20 (right) BERGAMO, Colleoni Chapel, the rose window. The repertory of ornamental motifs, consoles, bolsters, scale grilles and the classical mouldings, dentils, egg and dart, usually reserved for horizontal mouldings, are also used to decorate the archivolts in the North Italian Album. Photo: Conway Library, Courtauld Institute of Art.

Medusa on the bronze Gonzaga vase which was made for the Gonzaga of Mantua by Antico da Bonacolsi *circa* 1483 and which is now in the Galleria Estense in Modena.[38]

Another more sophisticated putto, wearing a tunic with his left hand pointing down, and his right hand holding a fish (?) against his neck (FIG.4) derives from Riccio's bronze *Tobias with a fish circa* 1506 in the Bargello or from its source.[39] Then on the right is a winged putto, with wings on his shoulders and heels, holding snakes in both hands while he treads on a tortoise, one of the lost attributes from the drawing of Michelozzo's *Putto* (FIGS 14–15). Tilman Buddenseig demonstrated that the putto derives from Donatello's *Atys-Amorino circa* 1440 in the Bargello and he used the drawing to reconstruct lost attributes: the two snakes in his hand and a tortoise beneath his left foot.[40]

The choice of vellum for the North Italian Album was unusual in the late 15th century when paper was more commonly used, although its durability would be appropriate for a workshop manual. Its very durability was probably the reason for the Album's continued use by artists of the second half of the 15th century. The irregular size of the folios, which have been trimmed, and their format, some with rounded edges others squared, suggests that the vellum may have been discarded from a diploma workshop where miniaturists worked. This may help to explain the interest shown by the Master of the North Italian Album in the artists called the Putti Master and the London Pliny Master who were the leaders in the establishment of the *all'antica* style after Donatello and Mantegna in the Veneto in the 1470s, and who collaborated in Padua and Venice in the decoration of manuscripts and printed books. Their style has much in common with the Master of the North Italian Album.

The late fifteenth century artist of the second group of drawings in the Rothschild album, 'the Master of the Flagellation', shared with the Putti Master an interest in the work of Pollaiuolo, as we have seen in FIG.3. Early in 1469 the Putti Master reworked the print by Mantegna's school of Pollaiuolo's *Battling nudes*.[41] The Hercules myth, the only myth explicitly evoked in the North Italian Album, was also explored early by the Putti Master and his collaborator, the London Pliny Master, and features of their iconography are probably found in the drawings of Hercules by the Master of the North Italian Album.[42] The drawing of *Nessus and Deianeira* (FIG.16), for example, was probably prompted by a miniature by the London Pliny Master.

The drawing seems to show a misunderstanding of the story of Hercules and Deianeira. A faun satyr, who has no role in the story, advances towards the fragile centaur who can probably be identified as Nessus, who abducted Deianeira from Hercules. He turns to touch the foot of a tiny, draped, acquiescent nymph on his back. Similar fragile, elderly centaurs are found in the frontispiece of a Sallust published in Venice in 1474 and illuminated by the London Pliny Master (FIGS 17a and b). The centaur approaches a faun satyr and embraces him as he protectively stretches his arm across the body of a nymph on his back in a gesture like the one on the drawing in the North Italian Album.[43]

***Ornament***

The method of decorating borders with single motifs, like the sirens in recessed panels, and the use of trophy relief panels which are rare in Lombard decoration but which are frequently found in the work of the London Pliny Master (FIG.17a) and in the illuminated books and manuscripts of Bartolomeo Sanvito, is close to the Master of the North Italian Album.[44] They used the same repertory of classical motifs, deriving from Paduan art, popularised by engravings by Mantegna and by bronze plaquettes, as Giovanni Antonio Amadeo, whose architecture also influenced the Master of the North Italian Album.[45] One of the designs in the Album could be based on the scheme of Amadeo's Colleoni chapel in Bergamo of the 1470s (FIGS 18, 19).

In the drawing the building is presented as a square basement with an order of pilasters supporting a deep entablature surmounted by trabeated pavilions. The building is crowned by a domed drum set on a rusticated masonry drum. The overall scheme derives from the Mausoleum of Hadrian as shown in Marcanova's manuscript (FIG.5).[46] While the Master of the North Italian Album takes up the basic scheme of the chapel, and is plainly indebted to Amadeo's layering of decorative motifs in horizontal bands, he rejects Amadeo's idea of decorating a building with an accumulation of antique numismatic portraits.[47]

FIG.21 (opposite page) North Italian Album, p.3. *The east end of a church*. The juxtaposition of the domed, cylindrical building with a lantern against a flat wall decorated with oculi is reminiscent of the sacristies on the model of the Cathedral of Pavia.

FIG.22 Cristoforo Rocchi and Giovan Pietro Fugazza, wooden model of the Cathedral of Pavia. The ornament with vases and pinnacles, scrolled strapwork stretched over domes and resting as bolsters on top of orders is repeated in the Album. Museo Civico, Castello Visconteo, Pavia.

FIG.23 North Italian Album, p.1. *Polygonal building.* The little building derives from the sacristies on the model of the Cathedral in Pavia.

FIG.24 French astrolabic clock, dated 1545. British Museum, Department of Clocks, reg.no.1888,12-1,123.

23

24

25

FIG.25 Model of the Cathedral of Pavia. View of the interior of the crossing. The piers with half-pilasters overlaid on two full pilasters and the continuous mouldings forming capitals deriving from Francesco di Giorgio and Bramante are also found in the North Italian Album. Pavia, Museo Civico, Castello Visconteo.

FIG.26 (right) Pavia, Cathedral. View of the crypt which was complete by 1492. The melon dome is like that of the Canopo at Villa Adriana. Francesco di Giorgio probably described it to Bramante.

The fleshy symmetry of the foliage rising from an acanthus plant on the wide pilasters, which replace Amadeo's accumulation of ancient imagery, is repeated throughout the Album, and finds a close parallel in the frescoes by Angelo Zoppo of *The soldier between two columns* in the Museo Civico in Padua.[48] The repertory of decorative motifs and mouldings in the drawing is consistent with the motifs in the spectacular rose window on the façade of the Colleoni chapel in which the tracery of the traditional medieval form is replaced by classical details (FIG.20). Consoles with foliage bolsters like those of Ionic capitals spin around the rose on the spokes of the wheel, composed of an accumulation of decorated cylinders, with deeply undercut rosettes and scale grilles between them and the frame of the rose is composed from dentils, egg and dart and bead and reel mouldings which usually decorate horizontal mouldings in entablatures. The same mouldings decorate the arches in the designs for frames and portals in the North Italian Album.

In the design for a two storey frame five equal bays stand on a projecting basement decorated with panels containing rosettes and ribbon ornament, the order at the side being an accumulated order of plaquettes and medals with disconnected classical motifs. The 'Composite' columns with spiral flutes and plain shafts are separated by decorated rings, and are set on tall, decorated pedestals, which occur in a slightly different form in the architecture of Pietro Lombardo – for example in the monument to Nicolò Marcello, *circa* 1481–85.[49] The Master experiments with arch and trabeation, and shows the two solutions for the archivolt meeting the trabeation block, deriving from Brunelleschi, which Francesco di Giorgio recorded in the first edition of his treatise on architecture.[50] The consoles with the standing figures ultimately deriving from the figure on the keystone on the Arch of Titus, seem to refer to the musical figures which were commissioned from Bramantino for the Canonica of S.Ambrogio in Milan.

The ornamental language in the Album is consistent: single items of a limited range of classical motifs, satyr masks, lion's heads, bucranes, sirens, Medusa masks, breastplates, rosettes, helmets, *tabula ansata*, profile busts and eagles, are set into recessed panels, decorate surfaces or form plaquettes which are accumulated into the design of piers. Almost all of these motifs are found early and frequently in Lombard classical ornament after 1470, and they conform with Schofield's analysis of Amadeo's ornamental language.[51] Only the breastplate and *tabula ansata* panels are unusual. The breastplate reliefs which are repeated throughout the volume, probably derive from Mantegna's fresco in the Ovetari chapel (FIGS 11–12). A wide but consistent range of classical moulding patterns is offered – coin, braided laurel, rope, *guilloche*, egg and dart, bead and reel, leaf and tongue, acanthus ogee, anthemion, flutes and dentil mouldings.

***Links with contemporary architectural projects***

The echoes in the Album of Filarete's architectural projects of the 1460s have already been described in other contexts. References to the model of the Cathedral of Pavia suggest that the artist was aware of the latest developments in architecture in the workshop of Cristoforo Rocchi, a master carpenter and engineer who is mentioned in a document of March 1488 as having, with Amadeo, presented a project and models for the new Cathedral, which were dispatched to Cardinal Ascanio Sforza, with a request to demolish the old Cathedral. Earlier in 1487 Rocchi had presented a project for the rebuilding of the Cathedral in Pavia as a small-scale reproduction of S.Sophia in Constantinople, probably based on Cyriacus of Ancona's drawing of the building, a fact which confirms that copies of humanist material were present in his workshop.[52]

In 1488, Cardinal Ascanio Sforza, Bishop of Pavia and sponsor of the project, who had received the design in Rome and whose approval of it was not whole-hearted, had asked Amadeo to modify Cristoforo's project and he invited Bramante to consult on the Cathedral.[53] The early history of the model of the Cathedral is far from clear because the early references from 1488 to hastily constructed models, do not specify the material. In 1493, when Cristoforo Rocchi rented a room for the model, wood is specified for the first time as the material. After Rocchi died in 1497, Giovan Pietro Fugazza gained the tenure of the building site in 1505 and was given the task of completing the model according to a new project developed by Amadeo

FIG.27 (opposite page)
North Italian Album, p.31. A repertory page with cylindrical, polygonal, square, triangular or rhombus columns with parade helmets, deriving from Francesco di Giorgio's treatise.

and Dolcebuono, and the surviving model contains elements of both projects (FIG.22).

It seems that in 1488 they were still thinking of an almost central plan.[54] In the model as executed the nave is eight bays long, of which only three were realised. The construction of all eight bays would have involved the demolition of parts of the city and the model in part probably represents a utopian scheme rather than an actual project. The greatest architects of the day were invited to give their opinions on the construction. In 1490, after Francesco di Giorgio had offered ideas for the tribune of the cathedral in Milan, Duke Ludovico Maria Sforza invited him to go to Pavia with Leonardo and Amadeo to consult with the deputies of the *Fabbrica* of the Cathedral and examine the building.[55] During that visit to Pavia Francesco di Giorgio sat down to lunch with Leonardo and his associates.

The crypt in the apse and the sacristies were presumably part of the original project, but it is not clear whether the architecture of the sacristies can be attributed to Amadeo, who worked at the Certosa in Pavia from 1466, or to Bramante. Richard Schofield, who convincingly established the possibility of a close working relationship between Bramante and Francesco di Giorgio, drew attention to the similarity of the crypt with the Canopo of Villa Adriana in Tivoli, and suggested that Bramante's design for the crypt was probably based on information about it supplied by Francesco di Giorgio before his visit to Milan in 1490 (FIG.26). He had drawn the Canopo in his Appendix to the second version of the first edition of his treatise Codex Salluzziano in Turin.[56] The foundations of the crypt were laid in 1488 and it was complete in 1492

when the foundations for the sacristies were laid. Francesco di Giorgio, the only theorist of the early Renaissance to recommend longitudinal plans as ideal types, shows a building like the Cathedral in Pavia with a dome the width of the nave and aisles, like the church at Loreto by Michelozzo, and a Latin cross plan with the long nave like the executed model is also shown in the first edition of Francesco di Giorgio's treatise, presenting intriguing problems for evolution and attribution of the design.[57]

A drawing in the North Italian Album shows the influence of this model (FIG.21). The design consists of an elevation of the east end of a church with a semi-circular apse on a basement. The dome and lantern abut a narrow, plain wall with recessed framed panels and oculi and a lunette pediment. The bays are not connected to each other, a detail which could refer to the fragmentary state of the model. The segmental pediment, which is more than semi-circular, and framed by bolsters, rises behind the cornice, and is on the same plane as the wall – like Lombard Gothic prototypes rather than classical pediments.

The basement, with arched windows lighting a crypt, recalls the crypt at Pavia, as it was built with round windows by 1490. The marble diamond revetment was also planned for Pavia. The juxtaposition of the ribbed dome and lantern against plain walls with oculi recalls the sacristies abutting the body of the church as shown on the model; the lunette pediments, and design of the attic with rectangular panels containing oculi, are all found on the model; the pedestal above the façade and the fluted urn on volutes is like the pedestal above the façade of the model while the figure on the arch in Bramante's scenographic engraving *Street Scene circa* 1500 (FIG.28) recalls the crowning figure of the Redeemer. Vases enlivening the roof-line are also shown in the drawing of the façade of the *Certosa* of Pavia in the Raccolta Bianconi in Milan.[58]

The domed, hexagonal building with two half pilasters at each corner of the octagon, supporting an entablature which is stretched to contain the attic, is crowned by tympana, in front of a ribbed dome with a lantern (FIG.23). It too derives from the sacristies on the Pavia model and the entablature, which contains the attic, is analogous to the gallery above the architrave in the sacristies on the model. The design of the attic in the drawing with an oculus within horizontal rectangular panels is found on the panels below the buttresses on the model (FIG.22) and at S.Satiro in Milan where two half pilasters meet at the corners of the interior of the sacristy which was rebuilt and redecorated by Bramante between 1477 and 1490.[59]

An almost identical building can be seen in the background of an engraving *The Descent of the Spirit* attributed to the Florentine school *circa* 1470–90.[60] In the engraving the attic has been opened as a balcony for figures involved in the narrative. The same design is used by a clockmaker for the case of a French brass astrolabic table clock dated 1545 (FIG.24).[61] Two other French hexagonal clocks of the same type suggest that the designs originated in Milan.[62]

FIG.28 (left) Anonymous engraver *circa* 1500, *The street scene*. This is the first visualisation of the descriptions in Vitruvius and Alberti of the Vitruvian stage set. The engraved medium suggests an educational rather than theatrical function. British Museum, Department of Prints and Drawings, reg.no.1860-6-9-43.

FIG.29 (above) North Italian Album, p.13. *Cityscape*. The drawing adapts Bramante's design to a vertical format probably suitable for an intarsia panel. The trabeated Corinthian atrium on the left of Bramante's design is shown behind the portico with arches.

### *Geometrical columns*

Four 'Composite' columns (FIG.27) with circular, hexagonal, square and triangular plans are displayed as a repertory on a basement with designs for parade helmets between them. The draughtsman – our Master – is insistent on the topic: he shows the same repertory of column types as the piers for a bridge (FIG.4). Here (FIG.27) they are shown with different examples of antique or 'Composite' capitals which were also found in Lombardy. The 'Composite' capital with a putto standing on foliage which ultimately derives from antique precedents was also common in Lombardy.[63] The capital with a bucrane and cornucopia is Milanese; cornucopias as volutes are found in the Colleoni chapel.[64] The volutes of the capital on the triangular column are supported by eagles.[65] In the view of the Ponte Sant'Angelo (FIG.4) he shows the same repertory of column plans and in so doing he seems to quote explicitly from theoretical and humanist sources. Marcanova's manuscript is the source of the image, which is probably based on Filarete or Cyriacus's reconstruction of the mausoleum of Hadrian, and Francesco di Giorgio is the source for the blades of the bridge and for the geometric orders.

Square columns with abstract rather than figurative capitals are usually associated with Francesco di Giorgio and are also found in Bramante's *Street Scene circa* 1500, and in the attic of the sacristies on the wooden model of the Cathedral of Pavia (FIGS 22, 28). They are repeated many times in the Album. Some of the 'antique' helmets in the repertory of parade helmets between the columns (FIG.27) are also derived from those drawn by Francesco di Giorgio who shows identical helmets with a winged dragon and with a spiral snail shell in a drawing in the Appendix to the first edition of his treatise in Turin.[66] No antique helmets of this kind survive but the tradition survived in repertories like these which were repeated throughout the 15th and 16th centuries.

### *Perspectival devices*

Francesco di Giorgio wrote about geometrical columns and illustrated them in his discussion of regular solids, a subject which was reinvented by Piero della Francesca. The subject was popular in Milan: Luca Pacioli, who was treated with deference in Milan and appointed to a chair of mathematics by Ludovico il Moro, wrote a theory of regular solids in the first part of his treatise *De Divina Proportione* which was dedicated to Ludovico il Moro in 1498 and illustrated by Leonardo da Vinci; the third part of his book was a translation of Piero's *De corporibus regularibus*.[67]

Piero's reinvention of the study of geometrical regular and irregular solids which he derived from Euclid took the form of drawing the *mazzocchio*, a

Fig 30 North Italian Album, p.22. *Cityscape*. The temporary wooden steps, pushed asymmetrically against the basement, of the towering Serliana façade, emphasize the theatrical character of this design.

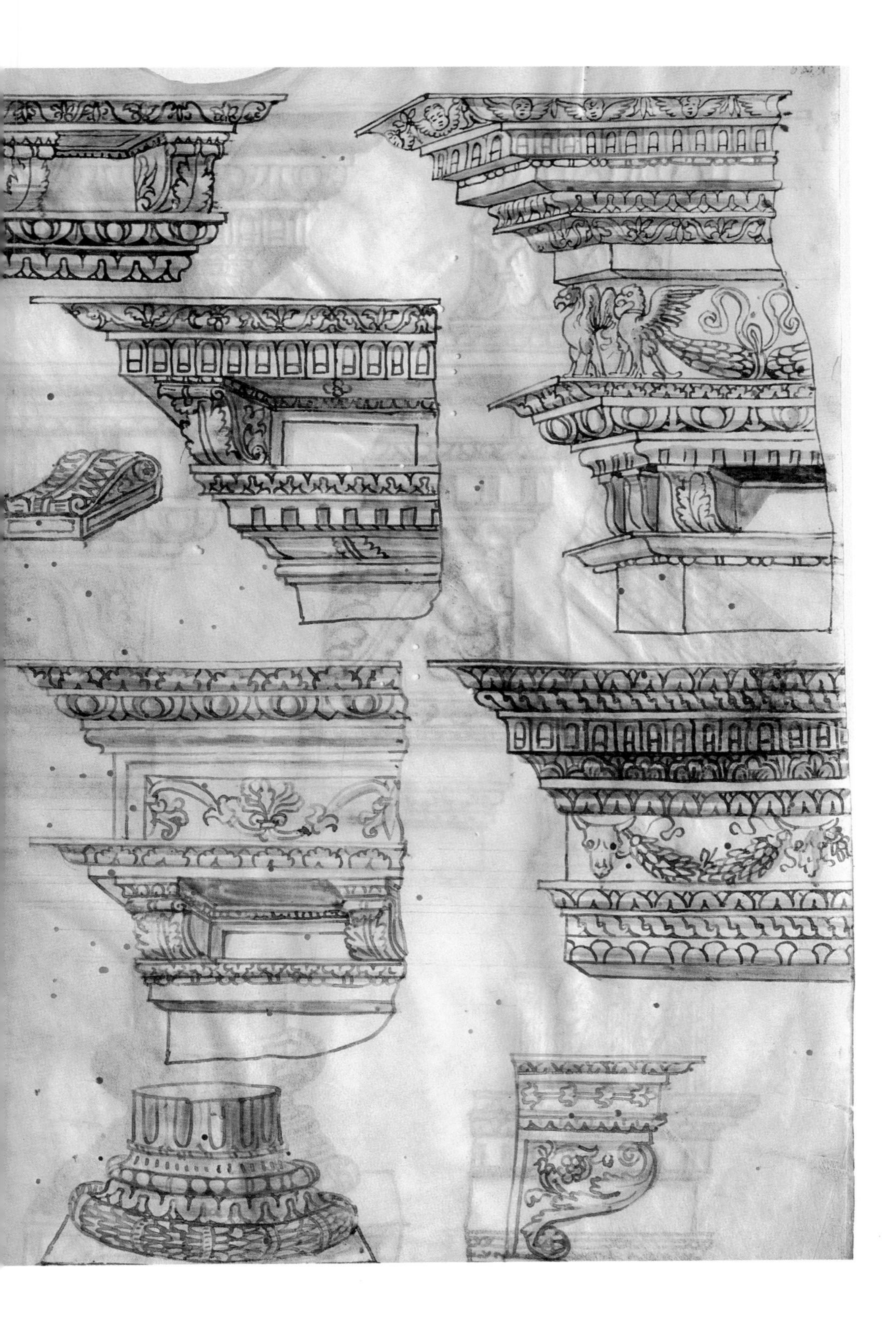

FIG.31 North Italian Album, pp.64–5. A repertory of capitals. The capital on the right with the s-scroll is a common Lombard type which derives from the pilasters on the second storey of the interior of the Pantheon. The cornice with the foliate modillions is close to Bramante's cornice at Santa Maria presso San Satiro; garland friezes with eagle and bucranes revived from the Antique by Filarete were common in Lombardy.

fashionable Florentine hat. He saw the exercise as the first step in learning how to draw architectural elements in perspective. Drawing the *mazzocchio* quickly entered painters' manuals as an exercise in perspectival construction, which was used to proportion perfect forms as well as the means of designing stage sets.[68]

Numerous perspectival views are evidence of the Master of the North Italian Album's interest in perspective and scenography. Pochat noted that the perspectives are not constructed geometrically; the vanishing point is often outside the scene.[69] The references to perspectival theory show that our Master was well-informed. The explicit quotation from Bramante's design for a scenographic engraving *The Street Scene* of *circa* 1500 (FIG.28) which, it is generally agreed, is the earliest representation of the Vitruvian stage set and is usually attributed to him, declares his acquaintance with the engraving. The corner perspective of the portico on square columns (FIG.29) derives from the engraving.[70] In the engraving the lower, square arcuated order on the right is contrasted with a tall, Corinthian, trabeated atrium three columns deep on the left. The Master has adapted the composition to a vertical format, possibly for use in an intarsia panel, by placing the Corinthian colonnade behind the arcuated portico. The detail of the perspective of the hexagonal well in the background belongs to a group of images which can be associated with Piero's *mazzocchio*.[71]

The perspectival effects achieved by Mantegna in his Ovetari chapel frescoes in Padua, especially the fresco of *Saint James led to execution* (FIG.11), completed in 1455–56 were greatly admired. The fresco set above the eye level of the spectator has a point of sight below eye level so that the spectator believed that the figures were enacting the scene on a stage just above the spectator's head, an effect reinforced by the illusionistic projection of the heel of the centurion into the spectator's space. The perspectival device, which was not Mantegna's invention having been used earlier by Antonio Vivarini and Giovanni d'Allemagna on the back of the San Tarasio altarpiece of 1442,[72] was very famous and Daniele Barbaro in the manuscript of *Prattica della Prospettiva* described the effect.[73] The frescoes were copied early: Marc'Antonio Michiel records copies in a house of a Paduan cloth merchant;[74] and it is interesting that the Master of the North Italian Album (FIG.12) reproduces a detail of the reliefs on the pier of the arch from this fresco in a collection of images which contain so many overlapping references to scenographic uses of perspective.

Milan was a centre for the study of perspectival construction which was led by Bramante whose great talent for perspective was influenced by both Mantegna and by Piero della Francesca. He was followed by Foppa, Zenale, Butinone and Bramantino. In the drawing (FIG.29) the architectural fragments in the foreground function as *repoussoir* elements for the perspective, one of the devices associated with Nicoletto of Modena which led Meg Licht to attribute the Album to him. But the juxtaposition of the superimposed square pedestal, cylindrical base and triangular core of the column like the frequent repetition of squares, circles and triangles in the

FIG.32 (opposite page) North Italian Album, p.5. *Metà Romuli in Rome.* The design could be based on the description in the antiquarian poem *Prospectivo Melanese* by Bramantino, where the conical mausoleum is described as encrusted with gems.

foreground of so many drawings, where they function as part of the subject of the image rather than as attributes of geometry, may carry an allusion to perspectival theory; they are evocative of the frontispiece of the poem about Roman antiquities, *Prospectivo Melanese* written 1496–98, which Charles Robertson convincingly attributed to Bramantino.[75] The conical shape of the building (FIG.32) suggests that it could be a reconstruction of the *Metà Romuli* which was described in *Prospectivo Melanesi*. 'Afrontallui era dequallalteze/ vna gran meta di pietra murata/ di gemme fine et di gran gentileza/ Nel mezallun allaltrera piantata vna pigna de octon coperta doro' (Govi 1876, p.15, stanzas 53–54) [in front of Castel Sant'Angelo, of the same height, a great pile, built of stone and encrusted with gems, on top of it [or on the other side] in a half moon was a gilded, brass pine-cone]. The description of the *Metà* covered with precious stones, is immediately followed by a description of the *Pigna*, the pine-cone from the fountain in the courtyard of old St Peter's which was covered by a vault on eight porphyry columns; the artist probably merged the monuments.

The use of the pigment in FIG.32 is suggestive of the jewelled surfaces mentioned in the poem. The artist used the azurite to give three distinct effects: with an undercoat of white it is applied thickly to give an intense blue on the balconies; it is ground finely and brushed thinly to give a green effect over the yellow parchment at the base of the tower and as a glaze over dark brown for shadow in the arcades. Other features recall Bramante and Bramantino: the exaggerated light effects that characterise many of the drawings are evident in the shadow of the balcony (FIG.29), the rock formations in the landscape on the right of the stage set and in the view of the Colosseum (FIGS 13, 30) is like the mountain in Bramantino's *Christ at the column* in the Brera.[76]

The extraordinary architectural perspective (FIG.30) shows a towering, free-standing serliana façade, which could derive from the Pazzi chapel at Santa Croce in Florence. Serlianas are found in Lombardy in the late fifteenth century; one stands above the choir at the Certosa in Pavia and Amadeo's use of it at the sanctuary in Saronno in 1507 is a late example. The serliana on four columns foreshadows Bramante's window in the *Sala Reggia* in the Vatican, and recalls Bramante's or Raphael's design for the nymphaeum at Genazzano. The double flight of temporary wooden steps, off-centred against the basement, serves to emphasize the theatrical association.

*A Summary*

As we have seen, the hands in both the North Italian and Rothschild albums, and their sources, are varied and complex. To begin with there is plainly a division of interests in the whole collection. The presence of early 15th century masters and two late 15th century hands in both albums who all record Lombard Veneto painting could explain the division of interests in the whole collection of drawings in Paris and London. The early masters recorded the Paduan and Venetian works of Altichiero and Pisanello and the anonymous miniaturist, who was the contemporary of the Master of the North Italian Album, copied works by the Paduan school of Donatello and Riccio, as well as Michelozzo. Works by the Putti Master and the London Pliny Master who were both active in Padua and Venice in the 1470s are copied by both the Master of the Flagellation and the Master of the North Italian Album. He could have begun his training with his contemporary, the miniaturist, in the workshop of the Putti Master and the London Pliny Master who as well as illuminating books, also made woodcut plates for the friezes which decorated the margins of printed books produced in the 1470s in their workshop in Venice.[77] The drawings made by the early 15th century hands and by the Master of the Flagellation in Lombardy, Padua or Venice could have been inherited by the Master of the North Italian Album and taken to Pavia where he entered a Milanese workshop.

In Pavia Milanese artisans, who usually belonged to small specialised shops, often forming consortia for large commissions,[78] were working on the marvellous carved and intarsia furnishings of the Certosa and on the model of the Cathedral of the city. In the city, the interest in architectural theory, promoted by the presence of Vitruvian manuscripts in the Sforza Library in their residence in Pavia, was not restricted to the humanist circles at Court, but spread into the building yards where copies of them were used by architects and masons during the consultations on the construction of the Cathedrals of Milan and Pavia,[79] which engaged the most innovative architects of the day, Francesco di Giorgio, Bramante and Leonardo.

The Master of the North Italian Album's dogged, awkward hand betrays a uniformity of stroke which is consistent with that of an artisan whose hand had to maintain an even quality of manufacture over a long period of time. His interests, as opposed to the themes developed and copied by the more painterly hands described above, show a consistent interest in architectural ornament and in the architects who worked for the Milanese Court. The depth of committed interest suggested by the consistency of the subject matter and the treatments within each type of image suggests the artist was a dilettante artisan, whose desire to draw far exceeded his ability. The quality of the thick line recalls the chiselled line of a wood carver. Geymüller's suggestion that Bramante made the album as a wittily crafted gift for an *intarsiatore* can perhaps be turned around. The album could have been made in deference to Bramante, the leader of the study of perspective in Milan, by an *intarsiatore*, a member of a trade which was so closely associated with the art of perspective that they were described as 'maestri della prospettiva'.[80]

For full detailed references to the drawings in the North Italian Album the reader is encouraged to consult L.Fairbairn, *Italian Renaissance Drawings in the Collection of Sir John Soane's Museum*, London, 1998, cats 1–67 (henceforth Fairbairn *Soane*).

1. Soane acquired the album from the bookseller John Britton in London in 1834. The vellum folios are folded and bound in an 18th-century marbled, Venetian paper binding. The title page bears a watermark, a crossbow close to Briquet n.738 which was found in the Veneto and Udine in the early 18th century. No evidence survives of an earlier binding. The sheets of vellum are of different sizes, some have rounded corners as though they once belonged to or were prepared for a volume, whilst others are square. It is probable that they were bound together for the first time in the 18th century in Venice, not far from the place of origin of the drawings.
2. Baron Henry von Geymüller, letter in *Transactions of the Royal Institute of British Architects*, 14 February 1891, p.93.
3. M. Rothlisberger, 'Un libro inedito del Rinascimento Lombardo con disegni architettonici', in *Palladio. Rivista di storia dell'architettura*, nos II–III, 1957, pp.95–100.
4. M. Licht, 'A book of drawings by Nicoletto da Modena', in *Master Drawings*, vol.VIII, no.4, 1970, pp.379–87.
5. G. Manni, *Mobili in Emilia*, Modena, 1986, p.70.
6. M. Licht, 'L'influsso dei disegni del Filarete sui progetti architettonici per teatro e festa (1486–1513)', in *Arte Lombarda*, nos 38–39, 1973, pp.91 –102. The Rothschild album is in the Louvre, Rothschild Collection, inv.nos 841DRR–860DRV.
7. Louvre, Rothschild Collection, inv.nos.841DR –860DRV. The Rothschild drawings also formed part of an album, which is now dismembered. They were acquired from the Sunderland Collection, formerly the Bonfiglio collection, in Bologna, which was sold at Christie's, London, 15 June 1883, lot no.67; Louvre, Cabinet des Dessins, *Dessins d'architecture du XVe au XIXe siècles dans les collections du Musée du Louvre*, 1972, p.9, cat.2.
8. Louvre, Rothschild Collection, inv.no.848DRV. A. Schmitt, 'Der Wiederbelebung der Antike im Trecento' in *Mitteilungen des Kunsthistorischen Institutes in Florenz*, XVIII, 1974, p.182, fig.15.
9. Paris, Frits Lugt Collection, Fondation Custodia, *Dessins Vénitiens de la collection Frits Lugt*, 1996, p.10, cat.13, pl.7. The figure of the soldier pulling up his legging on Louvre, Rothschild Collection, inv.no.843DRR is particularly close to the Lugt drawing.
10. J. Woods Marsden, *The Gonzaga and Pisanello's Arthurian frescoes*, Princeton 1988, ill.89–108.
11. In the entry written by Marzia Faietti in *Il Principe e Le Muse,* the catalogue of an exhibition held at the Poldo Pezzoli Museum in Milan, where the album was exhibited for the first time in 1993, pp.236–237.
12. Louvre, Rothschild Collection, inv.no.841DRV and inv.no.847DRR.
13. The drawings are on a light, creamy ground of the vellum which was prepared with lime and calcium oxide. They are drawn with a quill in two qualities of iron gall ink. The palette consists of vermilion, organic red lake, red earth, orange clay, organic yellow lake, yellow ochre, lead white, natural chalk and a very small amount of carbon black. The pigments are mixed as watercolours. Blacks, brown and beiges are achieved by different dispersions of ink. The colours are occasionally used on their own, for example the red tiles on f.8 are pure vermilion, the dense white on fol.5 is a thick layer of lead carbonate white, but generally they have been mixed and the mixtures seem to have been selected to achieve maximum transparency without losing brightness.
14. In a small city like Mantua, which was ruled by the Gonzagas, pattern books were often Court property which circulated between the artisans.
15. For the Master of the Mantegna sketchbook L. Leoncini, *Il codice detto del Mantegna. Codex Destailleur Oz 111 della Kunstbibliothek di Berlino*, Rome, 1993.
16. A.M.Hind, *Early Italian engravings. Part I Florentine engravings and anonymous prints of other schools*, 4 vols, New York and London, 1938, vol.I p.126, cat.13, vol.III, pl.185.
17. British Museum, Department of Clocks, reg.no.1888.12.1.123. Other clocks based on the same model and decorated with ornamental motifs found in the Album suggest that the connection between the French clocks is more than casual; Milan was occupied by the French in 1499. See Fairbairn, *Soane*, 1998, cat.1.
18. The Sforza often bought their gifts in shops rather than have them specially made. E.S. Welch, *Art and Authority in Renaissance Milan*, New Haven, London, 1995, p.246.
19. G. Chittolini, 'Dagli Sforza alle dominazione straniere', in J. Shell and L. Castelfranchi, editors, in *Giovanni Antonio Amadeo: scultura e architettura del suo tempo*, 1993, pp.19–43, p.25; translated Welch op.cit. 1995, p.268.
20. Giovanni Marcanova began the fair copy of his collection of inscriptions in Cesena in 1457 and finished it in Bologna in 1460: C.Mitchell, 'Felice Feliciano Antiquarius', in *Proceedings of the British Academy*, vol.XLVII, 1961, pp.197–223.
21. Modena, Biblioteca Estense, MS.992. It was begun in Padua and completed in Bologna 1st October 1465 and was not delivered to the dedicatee who died in 1465: C. Mitchell, op.cit. 1961, p.208.
22. Rovetta found the same source operating in the design of stained glass and manuscript illumination in Milan: A. Rovetta, 'La cultura antiquaria a Milano negli anni settanta del quattrocento', in *Giovanni Antonio Amadeo: scultura e architettura del suo tempo*, editors J. Shell and L.Castelfranchi, Milan 1993, pp.323–420.
23. The fresco was destroyed in a bombing raid in 1944. Mantegna was in Padua from 1440 until 1460 as the apprentice of Squarcione before he contracted with Niccolò Pizzolo to paint the left half of the chapel.
24. R. Lightbown, *Mantegna with a complete catalogue of the paintings, drawings and prints*, Oxford, 1986, fig.14.
25. M. Lazzaroni and L. Muñoz. *Filarete scultore e architetto del secolo XV*, Rome, 1908, tav.III.
26. G.F. Hill and G. Pollard, *Medals from the Samuel H. Kress Collection. Renaissance medals at the National Gallery of Art*, London, 1967, p.26, cat.115. For the interpretation of the medal as the Sforza Mausoleum, L. Giordano, 'Il trattato del Filarete e l'architettura Lombarda', in *Les traités d'architecture de la Renaissance. Actes du Colloques tenue à Tours 1er au 11 juillet*, 1981, Paris 1988, pp.124–126.
27. Filarete's manuscript is in Florence, Biblioteca Centrale Nazionale di Firenze, Codex Magliabecchiano II.I.140; another copy made for Mattia Corvino is in Biblioteca Nazionale Marciana MS.lat.VIII.2. A.M. Finoli and L. Grassi, *Antonio Averlino detto il Filarete: trattato di architettura*, Milan, il Polifilo, 1972, pp.CVII[8]CVIII, and pp.CXII[8]CXIII.
28. There are two versions of the plaquette, one in silver

is in the Louvre, Département des Objets d'Art; the other version in bronze is in the Samuel H. Kress Collection, in the National Gallery, Washington.

29. For the putto and garland frieze which was popular in Florence and with Filarete, see A. Burnett and R. V. Schofield's 'Accents decorating the Colleoni Chapel', forthcoming.

30. I. Hyman, 'Examining a fifteenth century 'Tribute' to Florence', in *Art the ape of nature. Studies in honour of H. W. Janson*, New York, 1981, pp.105–126.

31. Finoli and Grassi 1972, op.cit., fol.108r, tav.82.

32. Hyman 1981, op.cit., pp.112–114.

33. Rothlisberger 1957, op.cit. p.97, fig.3, related the building in this drawing to Sperandio's medal.

34. Traditionally attributed as Venetian, W.von Bode, *Collection of the J. Pierpont Morgan. Bronzes of the Renaissance and subsequent periods,* 1910, iii, tav.xxx, cat.181, p.21. For the attribution to Michelozzo, L. Camins, *Renaissance annd Baroque bronzes from the Abbott Guggenheim Collection.* Catalogue of an exhibition at the Fine Art Museum of San Francisco, San Francisco, 1988, cat.1, pp.14–16.

35. A putto, without sandals, with braided hair holding an orb in the fresco of *The Banquet of the Gods* on the ceiling of the *Sala di Psiche* in the Farnesina probably derives from the same putto or from its source.

36. C. Avery, 'Donatello's Madonnas reconsidered,' in *Apollo*, cxxiv, September, 1986, pp.174–182. Paul Joannides suggested that the relief is the source for the spatial arrangement of Massaccio's Madonna and child in the *Pisa Altar*. P. Joannides, 'Masaccio, Masolino and 'minor' sculpture,' in *Paragone*, no.451, 1987, pp.12–13, figs 15a, 18a, 19a and 19b.

37. L. Planiscig, *Andrea Riccio*, Vienna, 1926, pp.30 and 394–395, Abb.20 and 488, 491, 492.

38. London, Victoria and Albert Museum, *The splendours of the Gonzaga*, catalogue of an exhibition, London, 1981, p.133, cat.51.

39. Planiscig op.cit. 1926, p.197, Abb.224. Riccio, b. Trent 1470, d. Padua 1532 worked in small scale in terracotta and bronze making statuettes, plaquettes and domestic goods like ink stands and was an intermediary for the tradition of Donatello which he learned from Bellano.

40. Tilman Buddenseig used the drawing to reconstruct the iconography of Donatello's statue in 'Donatellos Knabe mit den Schlangen', in *Forma et subtilitas. Festschrift für Wolfgang Schöne*, editors Wilhelm Schlink and Martin Sperlich, Berlin, New York, 1986, pp.43–9, taf.xii, Abb.28. The tortoise below the feet of the putto could have been annotated in error below the feet of the *Atys.* Rosenauer summarised the various interpretations of the bronze 1993, pp.191–92, cat.42.

41. L. Armstrong Anderson, 'Copies of Pollaiuolo's battling nudes', in *The Art Quarterly*, vol.xxxi, 1968, pp.156–157.

42. L. Armstrong, *Renaissance miniature painters and classical imagery. The Master of the putti and his Venetian workshop*, London, 1981, p.59 ff., figs 42–47 and 73–85.

43. The John Rylands University Library, University of Manchester, inc.no.10547. see L. Armstrong, op.cit. 1981, fig.89, cat.37.

44. L. Armstrong, op.cit. 1981, fig.108 for Bartolomeo Sanvito, E. Schroter, 'Eine unveröffentlichte Sueton-Handschrift in Göttingen aus dem Atelier des Bartolomeo Sanvito; zur Sueton-Illustration des 15 Jahrnunderts in Padua ind Rom', in *Jahrbuch der Berliner Museen*, 1987–88, Abb.30–31.

45. Richard Schofield and Andrew Burnett analysed Amadeo's ornamental style and recognised the relationship with the Putto Master but noted that Amadeo remained in Milan for all of his career and it is therefore difficult to make a connection between them in 'Accents Decorating the Colleoni Chapel'.

46. Rome, Musei Capitolini, op.cit. 1988, cat.1, f.38.

47. R.V. Schofield and A. Burnett in 'The Medallions of the Basamento of the Certosa di Pavia. Sources and Influence', in *Arte Lombarda,* 120, 1997, pp.5–28.

48. Padua, Palazzo della Ragione, *Dopo Mantegna*, catalogue of an exhibition, Milan 1976, pp.22–3, cat.4b.

49. J. McAndrew, *Venetian architecture of the early Renaissance*, Cambridge, Mass, 1980, p.127, pl.9.9.

50. See Fairbairn, *Soane*, 1998, cat.96.

51. R.V. Schofield, 'Avoiding Rome: an introduction to Lombard Sculptors and the Antique', in *Arte Lombarda*, no.100, 1992, pp.29–44, and 'Amadeo's system' in *Giovanni Antonio Amadeo: scultura e architettura del suo tempo*, editors J. Shell and L. Castelfranchi, Milan, 1993, pp.125–156.

52. A. Bruschi, 'Orientamento di gusto e indicazione di teoria in alcuni disegni archiettonici del Quattrocento', in *Quaderni dell'Istituto di Storia dell'Architettura*, series xiv, fasc.79–84, 1967, p.44.

53. F. Malaguzzi Valeri, *La Corte di Ludovico il Moro. vol.ii, Bramante e Leonardo*, 1915, p.83.

54. A. Weege, 'La ricostruzione del progetto di Bramante per il Duomo di Pavia', in *Arte Lombarda*, 1988, nos 86–87, pp.137–140.

55. The documents are transcribed in full in R.V. Schofield, J. Shell, G.Sironi editors, *Giovanni Antonio Amadeo. Documents/I Documenti*, Como, 1989, docs 209–211, pp.183–184.

56. R.V. Schofield, 'Florentine and Roman elements in Bramante's Milanese Architecture, in Florence and Milan. Comparisons and Relations'. Acts of two conferences held at Villa I Tatti, Florence, 1982 and 1984, edited by S. Bertelli, N. Rubinstein and H.C. Smyth, Florence 1989, pp.201–22.

57. See Fairbairn, *Soane*, 1998, cat.94.

58. Raccolta Bianconi, vol.vi, f.36 illustrated A. Bruschi, *Bramante architetto*, Bari, 1969, fig.15.

59. Codex Saluzziano fol.93v. see C. Maltese, editor, *Francesco di Giorgio Martini Trattati di architettura ingegneria e arte militare*, vol.i, 1967, tav.174.

60. Hind 1938, iii, pl.185, cat.1, p.126, b1, cat.13.

61. British Museum reg.no.1888, 12-1,123.

62. Fairbairn, *Soane*, 1998, cat.1.

63. E. von Mercklin, *Antike figural Kapitelle*, Berlin, 1962, p.458a.

64. Communication Richard Schofield.

65. A similar capital, deriving from an antique example, is drawn in Codex Escurialensis f.20v H. Egger, *Codex Escurialensis–Ein Skizzenbuch aus der Werkstatt Domenico Ghirlandaio*, 2 vols, Vienna, facsimile 1905, text 1906, p.82, f.20v; for antique precedents E. von Mercklin, op.cit., 1962, fig.571a.

66. Illustrated by C. Maltese. editor, *Francesco di Giorgio. Trattati di architettura, ingegneria e arte militare*, 2 vols, il Polifilo, Milan, 1967, vol.i, tav.178.

67. There are two surviving manuscripts, one in Bibliothèque Publique et Universitaire of Geneva and the other in Biblioteca Ambrosiana in Milan reproduced in *De Divina Proportione di Luca Pacioli Tavola e testo di Luca Pacioli* in the series *Fontes Ambrosiani In lucem editi cura et studio Bibliotecae Ambrosianae*, xxxi, Milan, 1956.

68. Daniele Barbaro who used a ribbon *mazzocchio* as an insignia linked the study of perspective with scenography in his preface to *La prattica della Prospettiva*, Venice, 1568 in which he wrote 'Tra molte belle e illustri parti della Perspectiva, una ven'hà la quale da Greci è detta Scenografia'.

69. G. Pochat, op.cit. 1990, pp.270– 271.
70. Hind 1948, VI, pl.635.
71. M. Daly-Davies, 'Carpaccio and the perspective of regular bodies', in *Prospettiva Rinascimentale: codificazioni e trasgressioni*, Milan, 1980, pp.190–3.
72. R. Lightbown, op.cit. 1986, p.45.
73. The description is not included in the shortened version published in 1569. A. Morelli published the manuscript in *Anonimo Morelliano* 1800, pp.142–43.
74. For Michiel's description, A. Morelli, *Anonimo Morelliano* 1884, p.74.226. According to Lightbown the copy of *St James led to execution* survives, op.cit. 1986, p.400.
75. C. Robertson, 'Bramantino: prospectivo melanese depictore', in *Giovanni Antonio Amadeo: scultura e architettura del suo tempo*, editors J. Shell and A. Castelfranchi, 1993, p.377ff.; for allegories of geometry, M. Winner, 'Disputa und Schule con Athen', in *Raffaello a Roma*, acts of a conference, 1983, Rome, 1986, pp.37–38, tav.XVII–XIX). Bramantino, Bartolomeo Suardi, b. Milan (?) *circa* 1465; d.Milan 1530, assumed the name Bramantino very early indicating his close contact with Bramante. His interest in perspective and the dramatic use of light derives from Bramante. His treatise on architecture was published by W. Suida, *Bramante Pittore e il Bramantino*, Milan, 1953, pp.129–131.
76. G.A. Mulazzani, *L'opera completa di Bramantino e Bramante*, Milan, 1978, tav.I–II.
77. L. Armstrong op.cit. 1981, pp.26–29.
78. For consortia of artisans in Milan see E.S. Welch op.cit. p.252 ff.
79. A. Rovetta, 'Cultura e codici virtruviani nel primo Rinascimento Milanese', in *Arte Lombarda*, vol.60, 1981, pp.9–14, especially p.12 ff.
80. See the list of the Florentine members of the trade made by Benedetto Dei in G.C. Romby, *Descrizione e rappresentazione della Città di Firenze nel XV secolo*, Florence, 1976, p.73.


***Photographic credits***

Azimuth Editions, Sir John Soane's Museum and the author wish to thank the following institutions, who have kindly provided photographic material for use in this book.
Abbott Guggenheim Collection, New York, fig.14; Archivio Alinari – Foto Anderson, Florence, fig.11; Arte e Libri RCS, Milan, figs 22 and 25; Biblioteca Estense, Modena, 5; British Museum, London, figs 24, 28; Cliché des Musées Nationaux, Paris, figs 2,3,7,9,10 (Musée du Louvre, Département des Arts Graphiques, collection Edmond de Rothschild, figs 2, 3, 7, 9; Musée du Louvre, Département des Objets d'Art, fig.10); Conway Library, Courtauld Institute of Art, London, figs 20 and 26; Archivio Alinari, Florence, fig.19; The John Rylands University of Manchester Library, Manchester, figs 17a and b; Victoria & Albert Museum, London, fig.6.